Original title:
The Lament of the Dying Orchid

Copyright © 2025 Creative Arts Management OÜ
All rights reserved.

Author: Benjamin Caldwell
ISBN HARDBACK: 978-1-80581-804-5
ISBN PAPERBACK: 978-1-80581-331-6
ISBN EBOOK: 978-1-80581-804-5

In Search of Light's Embrace

In the garden, I'm hiding,
With leaves that are soft and wide.
Sunbeams tickle my petals,
Yet I must bide my pride.

Oh, to dance in the daylight,
But alas, I'm stuck in the shade.
My neighbor, the rose, is laughing,
While I just start to fade.

I stretch and reach for heaven,
But my pot's a cozy trap.
If only I had a ladder,
To climb out of this gap.

So here I stand, a dreamer,
In this spot that's far from grand.
While blossoms bloom all around me,
I'm plotting my escape plan.

A Tale of Petals and Time

Once a bud of pure splendor,
I thought I'd steal the show.
But here I sit, all wilted,
With nowhere great to grow.

My friends, the bright daisies,
Got sun and a lovely breeze.
While I'm waiting on a miracle,
And swallowing my peas.

Each day I tell a story,
Of grandeur lost in the mix.
But nobody's got the patience,
For tales of fancy tricks.

So here's to my short moments,
In a life that smells like dust.
I'll make 'em laugh with my fables,
Or just shed a tear—maybe just.

The Orchid's Yearning for Tomorrow

Pining for the sun's kisses,
In this pot, I sit and stare.
Waiting for my friends to visit,
Oh, how I wish to share!

My leaves are quite the chatter,
In whispers soft and light.
They joke about my roots,
And the way I cling so tight.

Every day feels like a Monday,
With clouds up in the sky.
But I've got dreams and wishes,
And I won't say goodbye.

Tomorrow could be magical,
With rays glowing all around.
I'll wave to all the dew drops,
As I laugh and twirl around.

Shadows of a Summer Gone

Once I basked in summer's glow,
Now it's autumn, what a tease!
The sun's slipped back to hiding,
While I'm left with just a breeze.

The squirrels are stealing sunshine,
As I sulk beneath the tree.
My petals droop in envy,
While they climb, so wild and free.

Here I sit with lots to ponder,
Like why I can't wear a hat.
Or how to throw a party,
With just me, a pot, and a mat.

But I'll think of bright tomorrows,
With giggles in the air.
Who knew that dying quietly,
Could be quite the comical affair.

Shadows Amongst Dusty Roots

In the corner where sunlight fades,
A flower whispers, but no one trades.
The dirt beneath knows all the jokes,
Of wilting dreams and playful hoaxes.

Petals droop like worn-out socks,
Giggles come from wooden blocks.
Yet ants parade with jaunty pride,
While orchids quietly bide their stride.

Laughter echoes in shades of green,
A sway of leaves, a quirky scene.
In their world where shadows prance,
They wink at time, caught in a dance.

Haunting Whispers in the Orchid's Shade

In the gloom, a giggle slides,
From petals peeking where hope hides.
Ghostly blooms joke with the breeze,
As roots wiggle below with ease.

A wilted laugh, a playful tease,
Swaying gently, they aim to please.
In cobweb corners old tales spin,
Of vibrant life and where it's been.

Each rustling leaf, a cheeky grin,
Though fading fast, they still wear thin.
In this dark, they charm with glee,
With life's little jokes, forever free.

A Farewell to Petal-Soft Charms

With all the flair of a grand debut,
Petals wave like they always do.
Yet time hits when least expected,
A shrug from blooms, sweetly dejected.

Chasing butterflies, a frantic spree,
Until they stop for tea and glee.
A final sip from dusty cups,
They chuckle quietly, then give up.

Charms may fade but humor's bright,
In dying light, they find delight.
A farewell wave, a jolly sight,
In soft decay, they hug the night.

Mournful Sighs of the Floral Grace

Amidst the sighs of blooms so bold,
A joke unfolds, though tales grow old.
With heavy heads, the flowers fret,
While laughter rings, the world forgets.

Curling leaves with ironic flair,
Whisper secrets into the air.
Their petals blush with endless schemes,
As dusk descends on fleeting dreams.

What follows next, a farewell dance,
In draping twilight, they take a chance.
The floral grace, though soft and pained,
Finds humor where the heart has strained.

Fragile Hues in Twilight's Grasp

In a garden filled with whispers,
A flower tries to sing its tune,
But petals dance like lost socks,
Underneath the lazy moon.

With stems that bend and creak like doors,
It shimmies and shakes—what a sight!
"I swear I was vibrant yesterday,
But now I'm feeling light!"

The bees all buzz with disbelief,
"Is that a blossom or a prank?"
As colors fade from bright to brief,
It grins and gives a hermit's wink.

Yet amidst the fading charm,
It chuckles with a wobbly spin,
"I'm just a star in fragrant arms,
In this garden, I'll always win!"

The Last Dance of a Withering Blossom

In the corner of the flower bed,
A bloom sways like an old-time champ,
"Why is everyone in such a rush?
Come join my clumsy hop and stamp!"

The petals droop like sad balloon,
Yet still it twirls with gleeful flair,
A dance of fate, oh what a tune,
Pollen flies, like confetti in the air.

"Is it sunset, or just my style?"
It muses with a giggle loud,
As neighbors laugh—a lively trial,
Inthis garden, we'll dance unbowed.

Raised on roots of joy and jest,
"I'll shine until the sun concedes,
For every wilt brings out the best,
In my life of giggles and weeds!"

Petals Falling on Silent Ground

Once a regal empress bright,
Now she's dropping with each tick-tock,
"Oh dear," she sighs, trying to fight,
As green ants plot and giggle, mock.

"Falling petals? Just a new trend,
I'm starting nature's ground ballet,"
She whispers to a passing friend,
As butterflies applaud her sway.

The soil laughs, a cushy bed,
"Drop more, darling, truth is clear,
We love the tales your leaves have said,
Let's party till the squirrels appear!"

With every petal hitting ground,
She spins in circles, wild and free,
Once lost, now found, she's truly crowned,
"Who needs roots to be fancy me?"

Memories of a Fragrant Past

In a pot with stories unwound,
A faded orchid shares its lore,
"Remember when I ruled this mound?
The bees would knock and beg for more!"

Now curled and quiet in the shade,
She mocks the gardener's gentle care,
"I'll just pretend I'm still a parade,
While you water weeds without a care."

Once a beacon in blossom's prime,
Now a punchline—we laugh in time,
With each wilt a memory spun,
"I'm still the star—just out of rhyme!"

So here's to flowers fading grand,
With humor stitched in frail design,
They wear their hues like grains of sand,
In gardens where the sun still shines.

A Canvas of Old Fragrance

Petals droop like tired clowns,
Wearing faces of fading crowns.
Once vibrant blooms with colors bold,
Now whisper tales of stories told.

The gardener sighs with a chuckle,
As he trips on roots with a chuckle.
"Falling leaves, the circus of fate!"
He can't help but smile at their state.

Each flower grins with hearty sighs,
As if to say, "Oh, how time flies!"
In this chaotic floral show,
They dance in dust, putting on a glow.

Yet through their wilt, a humor sticks,
Like a joke that never quite clicks.
In every wilt, a punchline's near,
A laughter blooms, despite the drear.

Beneath the Dust, a Hidden Melody

Once a stage for bees and cheer,
Now a quiet space, oh dear!
Cracks and dust settle like a quilt,
Yet underneath, a tune is built.

Petals crumpled, losing their flair,
Still sing secrets in the air.
A butterfly stops, gives a toast,
To faded blooms that we love most.

With roots that sometimes tickle the ground,
Their humor grows where joy is found.
"A lilac's giggle, a rose's sigh!"
Life finds a way, as seasons fly.

Hiding jokes in every crease,
They laugh at life, and find some peace.
Though petals droop, the heart stays light,
In this garden's fun, we find delight.

The Veil of Forgotten Colors

Colors lost like socks in a wash,
Once vibrant hues are now a slosh.
A gentle wind, a playful tease,
Whispers colors from childhood, with ease.

With blooms that chuckle in their sleep,
And roots that tickle, oh so deep.
They swap old tales of garden wars,
Over more sun, or just plain chores.

The violet hue won't stand for less,
Says, "I'll sparkle, in this dress!"
As laughter echoes through the leaves,
Even dust holds what one believes.

In a world where dullness once blazed,
These flowers wield hues, not phased.
A melody found in faded art,
Because humor lives deep in the heart.

Echoes from the Garden

In the garden, secrets still thrive,
Echoes of giggles come alive.
Amid wilted stems and laughter near,
Every petal holds a joke, sincere.

A daisy winks, "Mind the bee!"
Sipping nectar quite gleefully.
While lilies snicker, saying, "Why care?"
In their wilted state, they've much to share.

The gardener rolls in fits of glee,
"These once grand blooms are still crafty!"
Though fading fast, they outshine gray,
With jokes that brighten up the day.

So let them drift in the breeze's play,
With puns that never fade away.
In every nook, a chuckle brews,
As echoes weave through sundrenched hues.

Memories Bottled in Dew

In the morning, a drop will fall,
A secret shared, just me and it all.
Whispers of laughter, petals so bright,
Yet here I sit, getting sunlight fright.

Collecting the moments, all in a jar,
A lifetime of giggles, dreams that don't spar.
Swirling with memories, I'm still on the vine,
But this twist of fate, oh, it's so divine!

Each dewdrop a snapshot, like photos in frames,
Hoopla of colors, forgotten names.
Yet here I bloom, with a cheeky grin,
Taking life's jest with a little spin.

As petals unravel, I'll dance with the breeze,
Modeled in humor, I'll tease the tall trees.
For in every drip, a story comes through,
A flower's farewell, all bottled in dew.

Autumn's Touch on a Fragile Bloom

As leaves turn gold, I roll my eyes,
Whispers of winter, their gloomy sighs.
Yet look at me, all colors amiss,
Budding with laughter, can't help but fizz.

With autumn's breath, I sway on my stem,
Wishing for sunshine, not dry little phlegm.
My petals are crinkled, but that's just a show,
A joke on the garden, I'm putting on glow.

Each breeze brings a chuckle, old songs that we sing,
They say I'm wilting; I say, I'm a king.
The squirrels steal my blooms, what a scene!
I'll laugh to the end, while they munch on green beans!

Oh, autumn, my friend, don't take me away,
I'm ripe with mischief; I'm here to stay.
With a nod and a wink, I'll soak up your chill,
A fragile bouquet with a heart made of thrill.

The Fragile Elegy

Here I stand, all floppy and bent,
Drafty old feelings, no energy spent.
Yet humor, dear friend, is my solid glue,
Echoes of laughter, while petals construe.

Mourning my moments, yet giggles abound,
Slipping on sunlight, I tumble around.
"Can I borrow your soil?" I jokingly plea,
While dancing on roots, so carefree and free.

Each petal in disarray, a comedic sketch,
Masters of humor, are flowers, I fetch.
I'm fragile but bold, in this wild garden play,
The punchline of life, it's a humorous sway.

So let's raise a glass, fill it up with some cheer,
To blooms in the twilight, who can't disappear.
We'll toast to the quirks of our flowery fate,
Making light of decay, the best way to mate!

Heartstrings of a Withered Flower

Withering softly, but oh, what a tale,
A melodious hum as I start to curtail.
Strummed by the breeze, a heart-toned refrain,
Each note a reminder, of sunshine and rain.

Heartstrings plucked gently, in rhythm they play,
Withered yet witty, I'll stand here and sway.
The bees fly by, with flattery sweet,
Dropping their buzz 'round my battered seat.

A jester in petals, I twirl with a laugh,
Life's silly pranks, my beloved staff.
Befriending the rustle, the crinkle, the bend,
Even in fading, I can still pretend.

So here's to the flowers, both wilted and grand,
With laughter as sunlight, together we stand.
A song in the garden, a dance with the hours,
For every petal lost, there's joy in our flowers.

A Solitary Leaf Falls

A leaf once bright, now drifts away,
It sways and spins, in disarray.
"I should have sunbathed more," it sighs,
Walnuts chuckle from the skies.

Once a star, now just ground fluff,
Cursing the branch for being tough.
"Why did I dream of spring's full bloom?"
As squirrels plot my garden's doom.

A warning cried from ants below,
"Don't hang around, it's time to go!"
But here I am, a lazy puck,
Blaming the moon for my bad luck.

Oh, dance with me, sweet autumn breeze,
As we both tumble, if you please.
I'll send a postcard from the floor,
And wish the sun would shine once more.

Enchantment of the Ending Season

In a pot once filled with cheer,
I forgot to water, oh dear!
My petals fade, turning all brown,
The neighborhood's got a frown.

The garden gnomes start to jest,
"It's fall, my friend, you need some rest!"
I wink at them, quite in despair,
"You're just jealous of my flair!"

The pumpkins giggle, lost in their dreams,
While I reminisce of sunny beams.
"Stop mocking me, I've got some style!"
They grin wide— "Oh, just a while!"

As frost creeps in with stealthy glee,
I dream of spring, oh let me be!
A final bow, with all my might,
A dance in the moonlight—in the night!

The Weight of Unspoken Words

Between the petals and the sun,
Lies a tale that's never done.
Whispered truths, no one can hear,
As I wilt, I hold them dear.

The daisies laugh, they're all so bold,
While I cling to secrets, cold.
"Say it loud! It feels so right!"
But I just mumble— "not tonight."

An inchworm slips with laughter sweet,
"Just embrace your fate, accept defeat!"
But here I linger, holding tight,
To echoes of the silly fight.

So here I'll sit, half-baked and coarse,
With one last wish for better course.
If only words could float like fluff,
I'd sing my heart—but I'm just tough.

The Fragility of a Perfect Illusion

A flower swayed in sunny glee,
Yet whispered, "Why not me?"
Each petal dressed in sheer delight,
Yet pollen dreams drifted out of sight.

With roots that giggled in the dirt,
They mused on flaws, the bloom's dessert.
"Oh, to be a rose so grand!"
But here I stand, not quite as planned.

As bees buzzed by, totally lost,
Each pollen grain paid the cost.
They danced on tiptoes, full of flair,
Pretending I'm just fine, I swear!

So here I sit, in a pot so wide,
With thoughts of grandeur trapped inside.
I wear my wilt like a badge of cheer,
"Hey world! Look at me, I'm still here!"

The Final Blooms of Solitary Nights.

The moonlight beams on petals faint,
With dreams of grandeur, I can't paint.
A single bud, like a laugh gone sour,
Hopes for attention in a dark hour.

I strut my stuff, but here's the joke,
No bees around, and I feel broke.
"Is this a party?" I think and sigh,
But no one's coming, so I just lie.

The stars above can barely see,
How much I long to be a tree!
For trees get hugs, and lots of praise,
But I'm just here, in shady ways.

Yet still I bloom, in solitary grace,
Holding court in this vacant space.
A flower full of funny plight,
Chasing daylight into the night.

Whispers of a Withering Blossom

In garden's nook, I took my stand,
An orchid shaped by nature's hand.
"A monarch here?" I said with pride,
But nobody showed, I just sighed.

Whispers curled on these frail leaves,
"A lovely life, but what's the heaves?"
With every tick of petals' decline,
I wrote a poem—mostly whine.

Sipping dew for my daily tease,
Imagining bumbles, those buzzing bees.
"Oh, look at me! I'm quite the prize,"
But nobody's here to see my rise.

So here I fluff my wilting fray,
With humor tucked in every sway.
A jesting bloom with tales to tell,
In gardens near, where I laugh well.

Elegy in Petals

With petals soft as fluffy dreams,
I joked with caterpillars' schemes.
"Fate's a prankster, isn't it?"
In whimsical woes, I tried to fit.

I dressed in hues of fading light,
Dreaming of daisies in my plight.
"Why not bloom in laughter's grace?"
Yet here I am in this mortal space.

Friends are few, the bees have flown,
I'm left to muse, alone, alone.
"Will I be missed?" I gave a grin,
As crickets chirped their tune within.

Yet still I rise, though slightly bent,
With humor wrapped in my lament.
A flower bright in the fading sun,
In ironic jest, I've just begun.

Melancholy in a Glasshouse

In a glasshouse, bright and bold,
A flower sighed, its story told.
"Why did I bloom, if just to fade?"
An orchid joked, in colors laid.

With petals drooping, oh so sly,
It whispered dreams of flying high.
"I'd trade my roots for a comfy chair,"
A laugh escaped, in garden air.

The bees all chuckled, buzzing near,
"You'll be fine, no need for fear!"
As shadows danced upon the floor,
The orchid grinned, then asked for more.

"If I must go, let's throw a bash!"
It wiggled leaves, with a dash.
"I'd like some dirt, and a funky drink,"
The petals twirled, in jolly kink.

Final Petal's Farewell

A final bloom, the grandest yet,
Said, "Life's a show, no need to fret!"
With winks and smiles, the petals sway,
While friends all gather 'round to play.

"I've seen the sun, and danced with rain,"
It exclaimed, not one ounce of pain.
"I'd wear my wrinkles like a crown,"
With cheerful twirls, it would not frown.

So here's to joy, and goofy cheer,
Let's cringe and laugh, and drink some beer!
With every drop, my colors burst,
In funny blooms, I quench my thirst.

Sorrow in the Orchid's Embrace

An orchid yawned, with droopy grace,
"I'm tired of this same old place.
Each day I stand, oh what a bore!"
As raindrops tapped, it begged for more.

"I wish I had a wind-up soul,
To spin and twirl, that's my life goal!"
It sighed so deeply, then burst a smile,
"In this glassroom, I'll stay awhile!"

"There's Ladybug and Mr. Bee,
They're always laughing, come dance with me!"
With twinkling leaves, it spun around,
In this odd joy, its heart was found.

The Quiet Fall of Grace

As leaves let go, with a gentle sway,
"Why rush to fade? Let's laugh today!"
The petals giggled in the breeze,
"So what if I'm not what I used to be?"

"Float like a feather, not a leaden dove,
Embrace the quirks, and rise above!"
In every droop, there's humor found,
It played like clowns, around the ground.

"If I fall down, I'll land in style,
A somersault might bring a smile!"
With every tremble, a joyous flare,
In the quiet fall, life fills the air.

A Tapestry of Loss

Once a queen in garden's glow,
Now she sighs in shade below.
Her petals droop, they start to flop,
Sipping sunlight, she wants to stop.

In whispers soft, she spills her tea,
"Why are all the bees like me?"
A wilting smile with pollen jokes,
She laughs alone with all the folks.

Flowers giggle, roots dig deep,
But she's the one who can't find sleep.
"Oh for a breeze to take my plea,
Or at least a sunbeam, isn't that free?"

Yet humor blooms in a fading way,
As she dances with the bugs all day.
In pot of dreams where laughter grows,
Even in wilt, a smile still glows.

The Silence of Blooms

In a garden where chatter ends,
A flower dreams of winged friends.
Silent whispers, no buzz in sight,
She twerks alone, that's quite a fright!

Once the chatter was a thrill,
Now she wonders, 'Am I ill?'
Pollen parties seem so far,
Where's the fun in being a star?

With roots entwined, she tells her tale,
"Do orchids possess sense of fail?"
Her fading charm, a clumsy dance,
Bees seem to miss their chance.

But in the dusk, she cracks a grin,
"A wilted bud can still begin!"
So here she sways, her last encore,
With laughter low, but spirits soar.

When Life Sips the Nectar of Remorse

She sipped the dew in merry glee,
"What's wrong with this life? Where's my tea?"
Her neighbors bloomed, she cracked a rhyme,
"I missed the memo about this prime!"

In the bright sun, she made a fuss,
"Don't let my petals be a bust!"
As bees flew by without a glance,
She swayed and tried to catch their dance.

With every sunbeam, stories spun,
A wilting orchid, oh what fun!
"Please stop neglecting the queen in me,
I throw the best wild flower spree!"

So come and join in this shameless plight,
Where laughter blooms beneath the moonlight.
Regret may sip at her frayed edges,
But joy's the nectar, no one hedges.

Fragility of a Silent Chorus

A chorus of petals, a silent hum,
Yet here she stands, feeling quite glum.
"Wait, is it just me? Or is it bland?"
She rolls her eyes, but thinks it grand.

In morning glow, she tries to sing,
But all that comes is a pollen fling.
"I blame the bees for my sad mood,
Who needs a buzzing attitude?"

The roots beneath chuckle and sway,
"Just bloom with charm and forget the fray!"
But still she sighs, a queen in ache,
"All I wanted was a bright cupcake!"

Yet life drips sweet from every leaf,
She finds a laugh in her own grief.
So here's to blooms that softly care,
Even wilted, they still dare to share.

Glistening Tears of the Garden Ghosts

In the shadows, blooms do pout,
A ghostly giggle, what's this about?
Their petals droop like sad old fools,
Yet they dance in breeze, breaking the rules.

Mourning for their vibrant hue,
While teasing bees that fly askew,
'Hey, we're here to steal your lunch!'
A nectar party, what a hunch!

Dancing softly, they wave goodbye,
To sunlit days and clouds up high,
'Forget us not, dear flower friend!'
But come fall, we'll all pretend.

So sip the dew, and join the fun,
As laughter grows in morning sun,
For even ghosts in gardens know,
Life's a party, not just woe!

The Unheard Cry of Fading Beauty

Oh, wilted bloom, what tales you tell,
Of selfies taken, oh so swell!
'Look at me!' you once would boast,
Now wishing for a ghostly toast.

Petals crinkle like old parchment,
In a sorrow-filled, leaf-wise garment.
Neighbors chuckle, say 'What a sight!'
To whispering winds, they hold on tight.

When your last fragrance does waft away,
You'll joke of who made you this way,
With a chuckle, you'll softly sigh,
'Beauties fade, but jokes don't die!'

So spin tales of your glory days,
As the garden laughs in cheeky ways.
With memories bright, they'll bid adieu,
To garden gossip, and then to you!

When Colors Fade to Ashen Hues

In a patch where colors used to reign,
Now shades of grey bring forth the pain.
But listen close, as roots conspire,
A comedy set in the fading pyre.

'Oh look at me, I'm now a sage!'
Whispers a petal, wise as a page.
'With fading flair, I'll teach you all,
How to trip on dust in a fallen sprawl!'

Despite their dull and dreary looks,
These blooms are frisky, with playful hooks.
'Hey sunshine, don't you dare be shy,
We're still the life, just a different spice!'

With laughter echoing through the weeds,
They share their jokes and secret creeds.
Fading colors but hearts so bright,
Even in grey, they dance in light!

The Quietude of Closing Petals

As dusk descends, they close their eyes,
Humming softly, with no goodbyes.
'It's nap time now,' they softly plea,
'Catch us later, if you see!'

In their slumber, dreams intertwine,
Of basking moments in sun divine.
'Hey bees, don't steal all our light!'
They snicker softly, with all their might.

While lullabies of garden glee,
Wrap tenderly 'round each weary tree.
'Faded glory? We'll play it cool,
Just wait till spring, we'll break the rule!'

So giggle on, dear blooms of grace,
In the quiet, there's always a trace.
Even in slumber, laughter plays,
As petals dream of brighter days!

Twilight Serenade of a Dying Flower

In the dusk, petals droop low,
The bee's confused, not sure where to go.
A bloom once proud, now losing its flair,
Whispers of wind, does anyone care?

Caterpillars dance on my wilted hair,
While rabbits chuckle, they seem unaware.
Photosynthesis went out for a spin,
Now I'm just here, counting my grin.

Worms gather 'round, playing cards in the shade,
Strategizing ways in which I have swayed.
"Hey sapling, pass the leaf snacks, would ya?"
Who knew my fate was a comedy saga?

As sunlight fades, I wave my last cheer,
With a wink at the roots, "See you next year!"
Life's quite the joke, or so it seems now,
In the garden's play, I take my last bow.

Sorrow in the Garden's Embrace

The daisies giggle, the roses blush bright,
As I wobble and tremble in dwindling light.
My leaves trade secrets, gossip aloud,
While I joke about hosting a funeral crowd.

Oh, sweet petunia, so brisk and so spry,
You dance through the breeze while I slowly sigh.
"Have you tried yoga?" the thyme plants inquire,
While I ponder if the soil's on fire.

The sun hides its face, what a trickster indeed,
As earthworms prepare my chic burial bead.
"Make it snappy!" I shrug with a grin,
"Let's all wear shades; it's a party, not sin!"

A toast with fine nectar; cheers all around,
For a flower whose glory is fading profound.
With laughter and whimsy, I bid my adieu,
To the world full of bloom, and its mysteries too!

Tattered Dreams Beneath the Soil

In the dark, I weave wild tales of delight,
Of sun-kissed days and whimsical nights.
But alas, my petals are tattered and torn,
And the squirrels skip dance, I'm sad and forlorn.

Once a belle of the ball, now a memory washed,
My friends reminisce as they're freshly squashed.
"Oh, remember her hue?" the daisies do jest,
"Now she's just mulch, an organic mess!"

I chuckle at fate, how absurd it can be,
As ants march in line, discussing my tea.
"Should we grieve her early or celebrate now?
That petal's got style—take a bow!"

With laughter as music, I embrace my decline,
In this curious garden, I manage to shine.
So here's to the dirt, my tattered old soul,
In laughter, I fade, with a newfound control.

A Fade into the Forgotten Light

With a wink, I bid the bright day goodbye,
As shadows stretch long like a butterfly.
"Don't mind me, darlings, just blending away,"
With a chuckle, I tip my hat to decay.

The insects unite, throwing me a ball,
It's a going-away party, don't faint or fall!
"Bring snacks!" I call to the critters around,
As I wiggle and giggle, not lost but unfound.

Through whispers of dusk, secrets exchanged,
In a fading old gown that's somewhat deranged.
"Remember the time when I blossomed so high?"
The daisies reply with a sympathetic sigh.

As moonlight bathes all in a silvery hue,
I slip into night with a wink and a cue.
No tearful goodbyes in the garden tonight,
Just laughter and joy, in my fade to the light.

Tears of a Blooming Heart

In a pot of dreamy cheer,
An orchid sighed, its fate was near.
With petals drooping, oh so sad,
It whispered jokes, though feeling bad.

"Why did I bloom for just a week?"
It pondered hard, then chose to speak.
"My life's a comedy—who can tell?
Yet here I am, beneath this spell!"

The sun laughed bright, then slipped away,
While orchids joked about decay.
"I'll turn to fertilizer soon,
And nourish dreams beneath the moon!"

A gardener chuckled from afar,
With watering can and hopeful star.
"Don't fret, dear bloom, your time's not lost,
You'll grow again, whatever the cost!"

Soliloquy of a Wilting Stem

A stem once proud, now slightly bent,
It spoke in whispers, full of lament.
"Oh, what a life to wilt like this,
One moment spring, the next, abyss!"

"I used to dance in morning light,
Now I just droop throughout the night.
With every breeze, I make a joke,
'Why does this leaf always choke?'"

The pot it sat in began to crack,
"Oh, dear, it's time to check my back!
You cannot beat nature's fate,
But laugh you must—it's never late!"

Friends in the garden shared a scoop,
Of wilting woes and puddle soup.
"Let's form a club," the roots did say,
"Of petals bright and those in decay!"

Fractured Beauty Under Moonlight

Beneath the moon, a beauty frail,
A fractured bloom, with tales to tell.
"Why am I breaking?" It asked the night,
"I used to shine, now I'm a fright!"

With twinkles in its worn-out leaves,
It spun a yarn of broken eves.
"'Why are my friends so fresh and slick?
Maybe I'm just a comedy trick!"

The stars above began to glow,
They chuckled softly, wise, and slow.
"Dearest bloom, we're all a bit cracked,
A good laugh's the cure—you'll be unpacked!"

Change is constant, a fact of life,
Maybe it's fun—less stress than strife.
So, bloom your best amidst the pain,
And crack a smile, you'll bloom again!

The Song of Silent Decay

In the corner of a busy room,
An orchid sighed amidst its gloom.
"Here I am, such a sight to see,
Singing songs of silent decree!"

With petals fading, a humorous twist,
It said, "I'm a comedian, here's my list!
Why did the flower wear a frown?
Because it felt so upside-down!"

Companions withered, but joined the fun,
As laughter echoed; still, they run.
"We're all here—let's have a ball,
We may be wilting, but we stand tall!"

"You, my friend, look a bit blue,
When in doubt, just bloom anew!
We're fading fast, but that's all right,
With jokes to share, we'll feel the light!"

The Lingering Scent of Farewell

Petals droop like weary bags,
Where sunshine fades and laughter lags.
Bees once danced in sugary flight,
Now they sip a bittersweet bite.

Oh, the gardener forgot to water,
Made the flowers sulk and totter.
They whisper jokes that sound like sighs,
As they plot their great goodbyes.

Roots reminisce of dandelion days,
When they strutted in sunshine's rays.
Now they're stuck in a pot so small,
Sipping memories with a gentle sprawl.

So let's toast to the wilting scene,
With cups of stale coffee, just to glean.
A floral farewell with a giggle and wink,
As they fade into shadows without a blink.

Heartbeats Between the Roots

Down below where secrets play,
An uproar starts at end of day.
Worms gossip, saying life's a riot,
While orchids blush at things they've tried.

A trickle of sap, like giggling boys,
Turns a frown into silly joys.
But here comes the gardener with a sigh,
Watering what's left to say goodbye.

Roots are tapping a dance with glee,
While leaves pretend they're just too free.
They chuckle at the passing flies,
With each flap, a joke that flies.

As petals curl in a hurried swirl,
They plot how to outsmart the world.
With fading colors, they share their jest,
For even in dying, they still laugh best.

The Quiet Grief of Color

A purple blush begins to fade,
While green thumbs sing a sad charade.
The season's laughter turns to sighs,
As butterflies share their last goodbyes.

Colors whirl like a painter's splash,
But the artist has made a last dash.
Now every hue is a soft lament,
Even yellow's in a comical dent.

Bumblebees wear tiny frowns,
As they bellyache through garden towns.
"Why so serious?" they buzz and tease,
While petals flop in the teasing breeze.

With twinkling eyes, they fade away,
Writing punchlines for the final play.
As twilight falls, they leave their show,
A colorful giggle, a silent throw.

A Bloom's Journey into Dusk

In the twilight, blooms puff and puff,
"I'm too pretty for this rough stuff!"
With droopy heads and sleepy dreams,
They whisper jokes about moonlight beams.

But shadows creep with a comic flair,
Telling tales of the daring air.
"Oh, look at us, so grand and bright,
Fading quietly into the night."

Roots are telling riddles, you see,
As they quirk around a dying spree.
The petals laugh through scrunched-up folds,
While sunlight sends its tales in molds.

So when the stars come to take a peek,
They chuckle, "We're still not so bleak."
For even in dusk, a chuckle can bloom,
A joyful farewell, illuminating the gloom.

Where Regret Meets the Soil

In a pot with thrift and glee,
Once stood a bloom, quite pret-a-porter.
Now it wilts, a ghostly sight,
Whispering jokes to the moonlit night.

Its petals droop with comical flair,
A grand performance, without a care.
"Why did I bloom in such a rush?"
A squirrel scoffs, in the evening hush.

The gardener sighs, with a chuckle wide,
"I bought you cheap, you should've vied!"
Yet the orchid nods, oh what a fuss,
"Next time I'll ask, is it just me or plus?"

With roots that twist like a funny dance,
Each fading hue, a misfit romance.
Still it smiles, despite its plight,
In the graveyard of blooms, it takes flight.

An Ode to the Fading Light

Once vibrant pink, now a rusty cheer,
Our dear flower laughs, despite the sneer.
"Did I forget to water my head?"
A punster in petals, no hints of dread.

Sunlight giggles, a playful tease,
As the orchid whispers, "I'm not here to please."
With every twitch of a leaf, it quips,
"Photosynthesize? I prefer dips!"

A banquet of dust on a sunny sill,
Where laughter grows, and the jokes still thrill.
"Why do they say, I'm on my last leaf?"
The orchid winks, "Please, don't be brief!"

In the final glow, it takes a bow,
A fading star, yet refuses to cow.
With a wink at the night, it shouts with glee,
"Next time, I'll bloom—just wait and see!"

When the Garden Sleeps

In twilight's arm, the garden snickers,
As petals drift like playful tickers.
"Why must I close when daylight fades?"
The orchid chuckles at its charades.

The worms whisper jokes, quite obscene,
"Best plant your roots where it's less mean!"
While shadows dance, with a polite wave,
Our flower ponders, "Am I still brave?"

In slumbering beds, the petals rest,
Dreaming of fronds in a floral fest.
"I'll wear pjs made of sunshine bright,
Tomorrow, Alert! I'll take to flight!"

Yet as the dew gleams, the humor flows,
In every droop, the mischief grows.
With night creeping in, it yawns with delight,
"Sleep's overrated; let's party all night!"

Diminishing Hues of Yesterday

Once a diva in a botanical show,
Balancing sways with an elegant flow.
Now the orchid mutters, "What's the deal?"
With fading glory, it tackles the feel.

Each petal droops in a colorful pout,
With colors that lie, oh so smartly out.
A butterfly laughs, "You're still a star!
Just add some glitter, and we'll go far!"

In the fabled lore of the soil below,
The roots plot mischief, with grandiose flow.
"Why glam it up when I'm just beige?"
The orchid recalls its once purple rage.

With comical flair, it leans back and sighs,
"Life's in the laughter, not in the size!"
And as it fades into twilight's race,
It laughs at the sunset—the best sort of grace.

Solitude of the Passionate Orchid

In a garden where nobody roams,
A lonely orchid sighs in its home.
It spreads its petals, ripe for a dance,
But all it gets is a passing glance.

The sunlight teases with golden beams,
Yet here it stands, lost in its dreams.
A bumblebee sneezes, oh what a fright!
"Dance with me, dear, I'll bring you delight!"

Because the rose won the fairy tale,
This orchid just hopes for a bit of a gale.
It practices winks, for all that they're worth,
Hoping to bloom into something of mirth.

But time is vapor, and petals do fray,
With each passing season, they decay.
Yet in its heart, a giggle it keeps,
For life is just funny, even in heaps!

Chronicles of the Stealthy Decay

Hiding in shadows, the orchid sighs,
In a floral world of cunning lies.
It slips through the days like a comic thief,
Not a soul notices its leaf's disbelief.

Once a star, now a passing phase,
Its color's fading like old sitcom plays.
It chuckles softly, still making light,
"At least I'm more fun than the tree on my right!"

Down by the garden's bustling crowd,
The orchid's jokes are not too loud.
It sways with laughter, though it may fade,
Stealthy decay like a jester's parade.

Yet behind the petals, wisdom it knows,
In jokes and jests, true beauty grows.
As petals wilt and wilts with flair,
The orchid finds joy hiding somewhere!

The Unraveling of a Floral Tale

Once upon a time, in a verdant glade,
An orchid grumbled, quietly dismayed.
"Why does the daisy get all the laughs?"
As it inspected its wilted halves.

It plotted and planned, a comedy sketch,
But while it rehearsed, it began to etch.
With drooping petals, it wrote its plight,
"I'm an upside down flower, that's just not right!"

The sun would peek, but would only laugh,
As the orchid puzzled out its own giraffe.
"This tall tale's uneven, oh what to do?"
"Maybe I should try being blue!"

In the end, it smiled, with wisdom untold,
Finding humor in seams, as petals unfold.
For every comedy, with a quirk it prevails,
Even a jest in a gown that pales!

Echoing Silence of Wilted Leaves

In a meadow where echoes delight,
An orchid grew, with all of its might.
Yet whispers of silence began to loom,
"Is that the wind, or impending gloom?"

With leaves that quiver like a soft ballet,
It questioned the universe in disarray.
"Why is this bud now a wilted soul?"
A riddle, perhaps, or a jest to console.

Around it, daisies danced with flair,
While the orchid stood still, grumbling in despair.
"Can I join in, or do I need a break?
Or is this grand plan just a big mistake?"

But with each drooping leaf, it pondered and played,
In the echoing silence, new jokes were laid.
With laughter ricocheting, it made a new vow,
To thrive in the echoes, whatever the how!

Echoes of Fading Fragrance

In the garden, I'm a fading star,
Once so vibrant, now I'm bizarre.
Where is the sun? I've called all day,
Maybe it's off on holiday!

Bees buzz past, they just don't care,
With pollen suits, like fashion flair.
I whisper sweetly, 'Come smell my brew!'
But they laugh and say, 'Naw, we're through!'

Rain drips down like comedic tears,
I stand here chuckling at my peers.
The tulips boast, with heads held high,
While I just sigh and let out a cry.

Yet laughter's what keeps me alive,
A smile's the trick to help me thrive.
So here I sway in this floral jest,
An orchid's fate, who knew it was best?

The Last Dance of Delicate Petals

In twilight's glow, I sway with glee,
Trying to dance, but oh, woe is me!
My petals droop like a tired mime,
Oh, how I wish to turn back time!

The daisies giggle, they twirl with ease,
While I just shuffle like an old tease.
They whisper tales of spring and cheer,
But I just stand and sip my beer.

Each breeze a jolt, each gust a laugh,
Why can't I join them in this craft?
Nature's party, and I'm a wallflower,
A wilting joke in the golden hour.

Yet I embrace this final show,
With funny steps, watch me go slow.
For in this garden, giggles abound,
Even in fading, joy can be found!

Shadows Upon the Sunset Bloom

The sun bows low, but I stand proud,
Casting shadows, a funny crowd.
I'm like a punchline without a joke,
With petals like a clown's worn cloak.

I make my friends snort and giggle,
As I attempt a little wiggle.
'Why so droopy?' the roses tease,
I just wink back with humored ease.

Out of shape, I flail my leaves,
Pretending to dance as the sunset weaves.
Their colors swirl, a painted scene,
While I'm just here, an awkward green.

But laughter blooms in every light,
In fading glory, I feel just right.
So let them spread their glorious hues,
I'll be the punchline, with nothing to lose!

A Heartbeat Beneath the Leaf

Silent whispers in the evening air,
A heartbeat hides, beneath the flare.
I giggle softly, a secret beat,
While nearby, the crickets play their feat.

With every sigh, I tickle the breeze,
Throwing jokes at the bumblebees.
'Hey, I'm not dead, just in a funk!'
They buzz around, in their pollen junk.

I watch the day swirl, then fade away,
With petals that droop, I'm still here to stay.
A comedian cloaked in green attire,
Telling tales of my sunset fire.

So here I thrum, in nature's embrace,
A funny heart in a fragile place.
For laughter's the remedy I hold dear,
Even as the end draws ever near!

Melancholy of the Silent Stalk

In a garden where thorns refuse to play,
An orchid sighed, "I'm wilting today!"
With petals drooped and humor askew,
It chuckled, "Guess it's time for my debut!"

The bees laughed hard, said, "Old friend, don't frown!"
"You're the finest flower in this whole town!"
But she replied with a subtle smirk,
"I'm just a decorative piece at work!"

The gardener gazed, then scratched his head,
"Should I water you more or just leave you for dead?"
"Just one last drink, then I'll throw in the towel,"
The orchid winked, "You'll miss me, old pal!"

So here she stands, 'neath the bright blue skies,
Waving goodbye with her wilted goodbyes.
In every petal's droop lies a laugh, my friend,
A comedy of life where all things must end!

Shadows on the Sunlit Leaves

In the sun's glow, the orchids play tricks,
Casting shadows, a comedy mix.
With flowers that dance and tease the light,
"Watch me quiver! I'm quite the sight!"

They giggled in whispers, then slowly bowed,
Fading away, they still felt proud.
"I may be wilting, yes, that is true,
But I've still got jokes for me and for you!"

The daisies said, "Oh, give us a break!
It's tough to bloom when you're making us ache."
But the orchids shrugged, with humor so spry,
"Every bloom has its day, now hand me a pie!"

So in the garden where silliness reigned,
Sunlit leaves where laughter remained.
Each withering smile and each petal so bold,
Makes life just a tale that never gets old!

When Beauty Meets Its Withering

Oh, beauty, you stand with your face in the sun,
But now you're drooping—oh what a run!
The petals declared, "We're too tired to bloom,
Let's start our comedy show from this room!"

With a wink and a twirl, they pranced in decay,
"Just give us a moment, we'll be on our way!"
A bumblebee shouted, "Don't you go yet!
You're still the best act that I've ever met!"

Yet off they would go, petals falling like laughs,
With "retirement" jokes the whole garden drafts.
So while beauty may fade, don't hang your hat,
There's always a punchline, and that's that!

And there in the twilight of sweet blooming days,
The orchids kept giggling in wild, silly ways.
They found joy in fading—how hilarious indeed!
For laughter's the root of every good deed!

Echoes of a Decay Untold

In the corner of gardens where shadows do creep,
Lies a tale of blossoms who forget how to sleep.
"Time for a nap!" whispered one, so coy,
"We'll wake when it's juicy, oh what a joy!"

As petals turned crispy, they planned a light snack,
"A piece of fresh sunlight, and then we'll relax!"
The leaves all conspired, "What's roast bloom for tea?
Let's have a feast, all wilted and free!"

Lilies and daisies rolled eyes at this sight,
"Quit squabbling, decrepit, you're not a delight!"
But the orchids just smirked, with a lightly toned grin,
"Hey, life is a banquet, we're here for the win!"

In echoes of fading, the laughter took flight,
For who said that dying can't lead to delight?
So raise a glass high, let it shimmer and gleam,
In decay, there's a humor—it's life's greatest dream!

Ghosts of a Blooming Past

Once I danced in sunlit rays,
With petals bright in fragrant days.
Now I sit, my soil all crust,
In search of water, but who can trust?

The buzzing bees, they used to play,
Now they flee, like ghosts, away.
Once I grinned with vibrant hues,
Now a shadow in sad, grey views.

When Colors Fade to Grey

In youth, I wore a rainbow crown,
Now my colors settle down.
What happened to the sunny glee?
Now it's just me and a wilting spree!

I used to shout; I used to sing,
Now I'm quieter than a sting.
With every drop that doesn't come,
I ponder if I've been outdone.

A Reverie of Lost Blossoms

I reminisce of petals bright,
And longing for a springtime night.
But here I am, just stems that creak,
Wish I could sprout a little peak!

The garden hosts a vibrant crew,
While I just sit in shades of blue.
Once a beauty, full of cheer,
Now a relic, disappearing here.

The Orchid's Last Breath

With every sigh, the vase does shake,
A final chance for goodness' sake.
I wave goodbye to petals worn,
In hopes that humor can be born!

Like a comedian's old, tired act,
I ponder if I was ever intact.
One last chuckle before I pout,
Perhaps my jokes are what's kept me out!

Whispers of a Wilted Petal

In a pot with not much cheer,
A wilted flower sheds a tear.
It whispers secrets of the sun,
While urging bees to just have fun.

With every breeze it rustles faint,
"What's left of me? A wilted saint!
Though once I danced in vibrant hues,
Now I'm the plant that sings the blues."

Roots tangled up like old shoelaces,
It cracks jokes on the garden's faces.
"I'm a legend with a twist of fate,
Consider me as 'flourishing late!'"

So here's to petals, slightly old,
Who trade their glory for tales bold.
In wilting charm, they find delight,
With laughter shared into the night.

Elegy of the Forsaken Bloom

In daylight's glow, the petals yawn,
"I swear I used to be the dawn!"
With chlorophyll dreams and a wistful sigh,
"I'm just a shadow 'neath the sky."

Once a queen with colors bright,
Now a joke with fading might.
"Roses are red, violets are blue,
I'm an expiring leaf, how about you?"

The worms chuckle, the ants have a ball,
While I sit here and slowly stall.
"Call me wilted, call me past Prime,
I'm the punchline of garden rhyme."

But still I stand, a smile so wide,
Trading my glory for humor and pride.
In every crack, there's joy confined,
In swaying leaves, a joke designed.

Ghosts of a Once-Vibrant Garden

In the corner, a ghostly hue,
"Was I not pretty? Did I offend you?"
The marigolds snicker and share a glance,
As crumbling petals do their dance.

"Remember the days of vibrant cheer?
Now I whisper to the deer!"
With every breeze, a soft complaint,
"Who knew blush would fade, not a saint!"

Potting soil jokes, potpourri puns,
Ghost orchids grin, under the sun.
"Why did the flower get a cold?
Spoiler alert—it's getting old!"

Despite decay, laughter rings out,
In this ghostly patch, there's little doubt.
With each wilt, I cheerfully jest,
In a garden of memories, I'm truly blessed.

A Song for the Fading Fragrance

Oh fading bloom, with scent so slight,
You giggle softly, embracing the night.
"I may not be sweet like a sugar cake,
But I bring laughter for goodness' sake!"

With petals drooping from all the joy,
Telling tales, a little coy.
"Once I was fragrant, a scented king,
Now I rhyme like a fading spring."

The ladybugs chuckle as they crawl,
"Who needs scent when you're the life of the hall?"
"I've got stories of pollen and bees,
And how I danced in the summer breeze."

So raise a pot, let's toast tonight,
To fading blooms still shining bright.
In every drip, a wink, a grin,
We'll be the life amidst the din.

www.ingramcontent.com/pod-product-compliance
Lightning Source LLC
Chambersburg PA
CBHW070333120526
44590CB00017B/2871